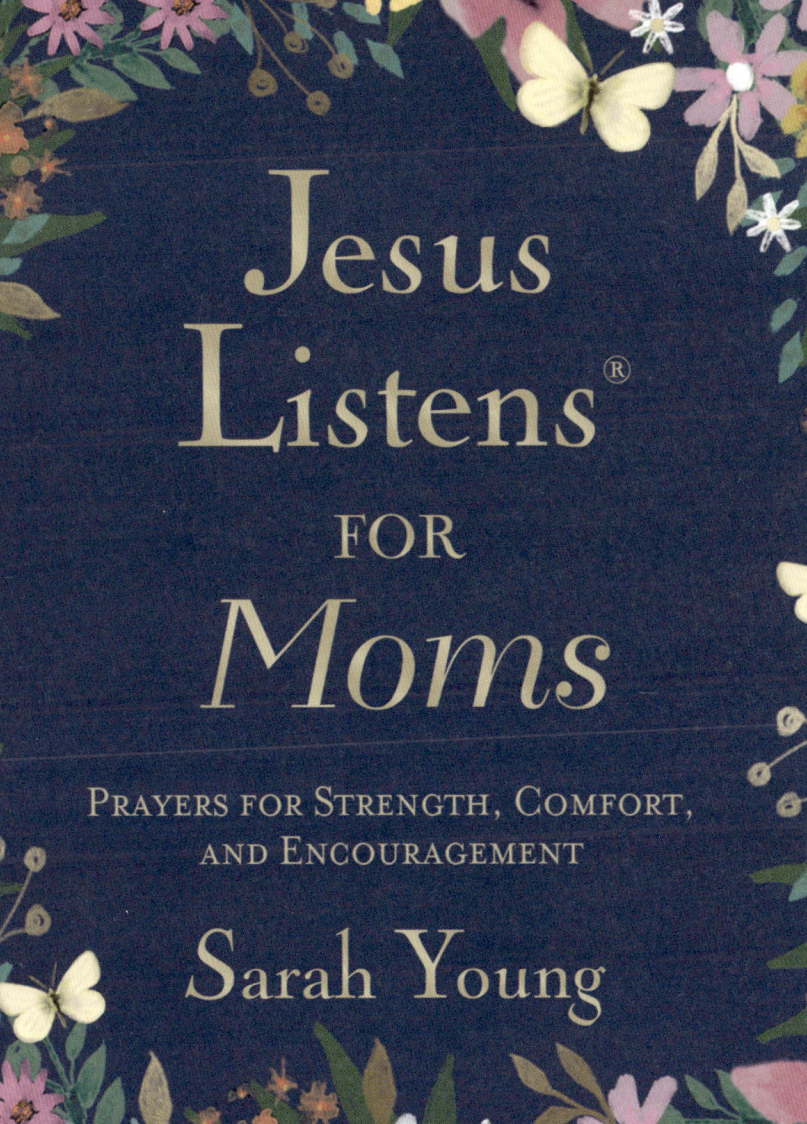

Jesus Listens

FOR *Moms*

PRAYERS FOR STRENGTH, COMFORT, AND ENCOURAGEMENT

Sarah Young

Jesus Listens® for Moms

© 2026 Jesus Calling Foundation

Portions of this book were taken from *Jesus Listens®* and *Jesus Calling®*.

All rights reserved. No portion of this book may be reproduced, stored in a retrieval system, or transmitted in any form or by any means—electronic, mechanical, photocopy, recording, scanning, or other—except for brief quotations in critical reviews or articles, without the prior written permission of the publisher.

Published by Thomas Nelson, 501 Nelson Place, Nashville, TN 37214, USA. Thomas Nelson is a registered trademark of HarperCollins Christian Publishing, Inc.

Thomas Nelson titles may be purchased in bulk for educational, business, fundraising, or sales promotional use. For information, please email SpecialMarkets@ThomasNelson.com.

Unless otherwise noted, scripture quotations are taken from The Holy Bible, New International Version®, NIV®. Copyright © 1973, 1978, 1984 by Biblica, Inc.® Used by permission of Zondervan. All rights reserved worldwide. www.Zondervan.com. The "NIV" and "New International Version" are trademarks registered in the United States Patent and Trademark Office by Biblica, Inc.®

Scripture quotations marked AMPC are taken from the Amplified® Bible. Copyright © 1954, 1958, 1962, 1964, 1965, 1987 by The Lockman Foundation. Used by permission. (www.Lockman.org)

Scripture quotations marked ESV are taken from the ESV® Bible (The Holy Bible, English Standard Version®). Copyright © 2001 by Crossway, a publishing ministry of Good News Publishers. Used by permission. All rights reserved.

Scripture quotations marked HCSB are taken from the Holman Christian Standard Bible®. Copyright © 1999, 2000, 2002, 2003, 2009 by Holman Bible Publishers. Used by permission. HCSB® is a federally registered trademark of Holman Bible Publishers.

Scripture quotations marked KJV are taken from the King James Version. Public domain.

Scripture quotations marked MSG are taken from *The Message*. Copyright © 1993, 2002, 2018 by Eugene H. Peterson. Used by permission of NavPress. All rights reserved. Represented by Tyndale House Publishers, a Division of Tyndale House Ministries.

Scripture quotations marked NASB 1995 are taken from the New American Standard Bible®. Copyright © 1960, 1971, 1977, 1995 by The Lockman Foundation. Used by permission. All rights reserved. www.lockman.org.

Scripture quotations marked NKJV are taken from the New King James Version®. © 1982 by Thomas Nelson. Used by permission. All rights reserved.

Scripture quotations marked NLT are taken from the Holy Bible, New Living Translation. © 1996, 2004, 2007, 2013, 2015 by Tyndale House Foundation. Used by permission. www.Lockman.org.

Scripture quotations marked TLB are taken from The Living Bible. Copyright © 1971. Used by permission of Tyndale House Publishers, Inc., Carol Stream, Illinois 60188. All rights reserved.

Any internet addresses, phone numbers, or company or product information printed in this book are offered as a resource and are not intended in any way to be or to imply an endorsement by Thomas Nelson, nor does Thomas Nelson vouch for the existence, content, or services of these sites, phone numbers, companies, or products beyond the life of this book.

Without limiting the exclusive rights of any author, contributor or the publisher of this publication, any unauthorized use of this publication to train generative artificial intelligence (AI) technologies is expressly prohibited. HarperCollins also exercise their rights under Article 4(3) of the Digital Single Market Directive 2019/790 and expressly reserve this publication from the text and data mining exception.

Art by Sally Wilson
Cover design by Sabryna Lugge
Interior design by Mallory Collins

ISBN 978-1-4002-5570-2 (HC)
ISBN 978-1-4002-5572-6 (audiobook)
ISBN 978-1-4002-5571-9 (eBook)

Printed in Vietnam

A Prayer for Moms

Compassionate Lord Jesus,

    I ask You to use these devotions to bless and help mothers—strengthening, encouraging, and comforting them as they go about their daily lives. Remind them that You are with them each and every moment, regardless of what is happening. Please shower them with Your unfailing Love, and enable them to love their children well. Help their children truly know You as Savior and Lord.

    In your glorious, victorious Name, Amen.

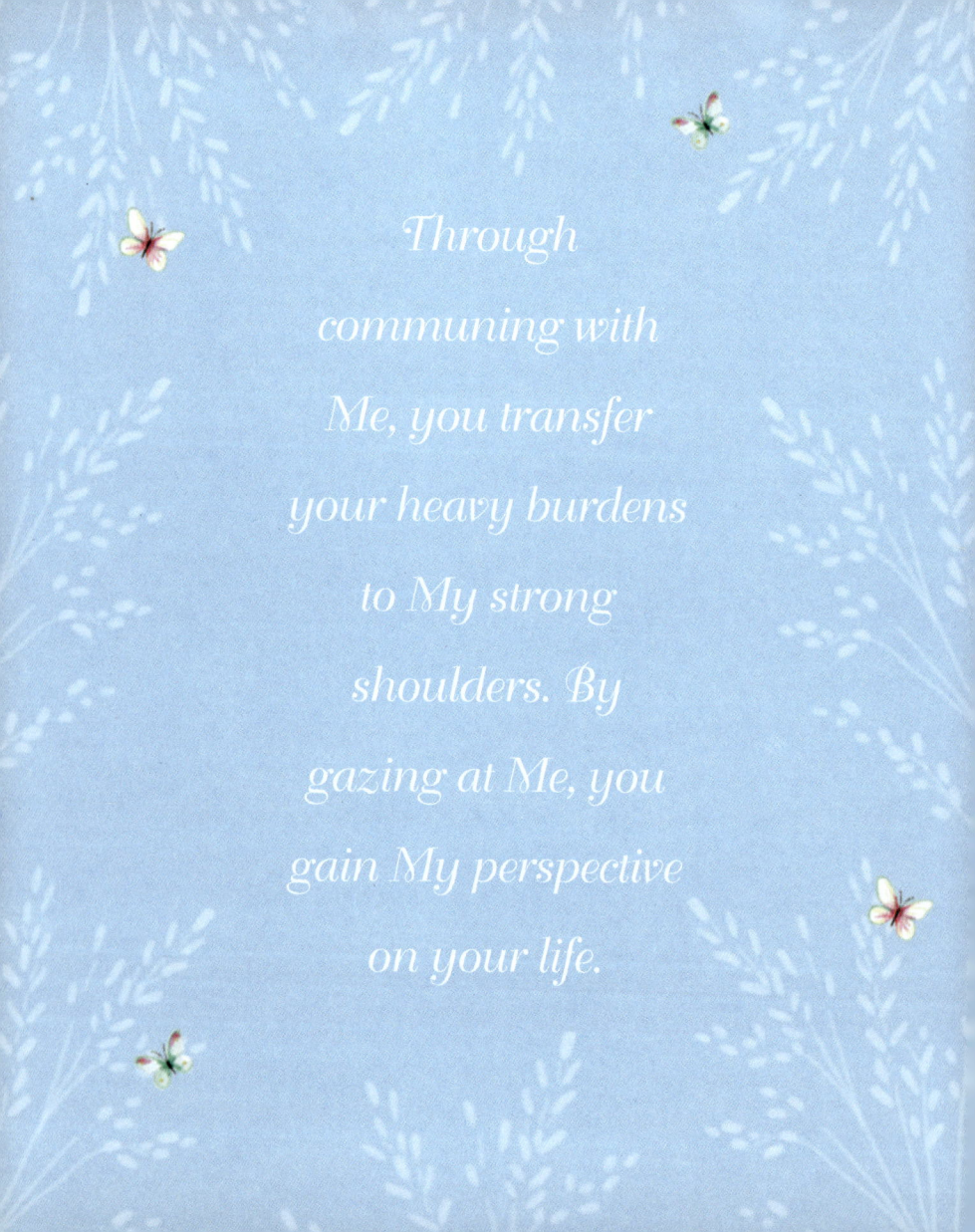

Through communing with Me, you transfer your heavy burdens to My strong shoulders. By gazing at Me, you gain My perspective on your life.

BEAUTIFUL SAVIOR,

I long to comprehend the depth and breadth of *Your Love that surpasses knowledge*! I've seen that there's an enormous difference between really knowing You and simply knowing *about* You. Instead of just knowing some facts about You, I want to enjoy the glorious experience of Your loving Presence. I realize that I need the help of Your Spirit—*strengthening me with Power in my inner being so I can grasp how wide and long and high and deep is Your Love* for me.

You have been alive in my heart since the moment of my salvation. I've discovered that the more room I make for You in my inner being, the more You fill me with Your Love. You've been teaching me to expand this space in my heart by spending ample time with You and absorbing Your Word. I want to learn to stay in communication with You more and more—*praying continually*. These are joyful disciplines, and they keep me close to You through the ups and downs of motherhood.

Lord, I ask that Your Love may flow through me into the lives of other people. This *makes Your Love in me complete*.

IN YOUR LOVING NAME, JESUS, AMEN.

I pray that out of his glorious riches he may strengthen you with power through his Spirit in your inner being . . . to grasp how wide and long and high and deep is the love of Christ, and to know this love that surpasses knowledge.

Ephesians 3:16, 18–19

Pray continually.

1 Thessalonians 5:17

No one has ever seen God; but if we love one another, God lives in us and his love is made complete in us.

1 John 4:12

My Jesus,

You designed me to live in union with You. I'm thankful that this union does not negate who I am. On the contrary, it makes me more fully myself. I've discovered that when I try to live independently of You—even for short periods of time—I experience emptiness and dissatisfaction. But *when I walk in the Light of Your Presence*, You bless me with deep, satisfying Joy. I delight in praising You—*exulting in Your righteousness.*

Help me to find fulfillment in living close to You, yielding to Your purposes for me. Sometimes You lead me along paths that feel alien to me. At such times I need to cling to You—trusting that You know what You're doing. When I follow You wholeheartedly, I can discover facets of myself that were previously hidden.

You know me intimately—far better than I know myself. In union with You, I am complete. In closeness to You, I am transformed more and more into the one You created me to be.

In Your beautiful, righteous Name, Amen.

Blessed are those who have learned to acclaim you, who walk in the light of your presence, O Lord. They rejoice in your name all day long; they exult in your righteousness.

PSALM 89:15–16

My frame was not hidden from you when I was made in the secret place. When I was woven together in the depths of the earth, your eyes saw my unformed body.

PSALM 139:15–16

We all, with unveiled face, beholding the glory of the Lord, are being transformed into the same image from one degree of glory to another. For this comes from the Lord who is the Spirit.

2 CORINTHIANS 3:18 ESV

GLORIOUS JESUS,

Help me to lay down my problems long enough to gaze at You. Sometimes I picture myself standing at the edge of a magnificent ocean, on a beach covered with pebbles. The pebbles represent problems—mine, my family's, my friends', the world's. When I pick up these small stones and hold them close to my eyes, examining their details, my view of the grandeur all around me is blocked. Usually, as soon as I put down one pebble-problem, I pick up another. Thus I fail to enjoy the beauty of Your Presence and the blessing of *Your unfailing Love*.

The ocean represents *You*—endlessly glorious and continually present with me. I want to put down *all* the pebbles so I can experience Your loving Presence. As I wait with You, I can almost hear You whispering: "Choose *Me*, beloved. Choose to see Me—to find Me—in your moments."

I long for the day when seeking You continually will be a habit—a delightful habit that keeps me close to You on *the path of Life*.

IN YOUR EXQUISITE NAME, AMEN.

Looking to Jesus, the founder and perfecter of
our faith, who for the joy set before him endured
the cross, despising the shame, and is seated
at the right hand of the throne of God.

HEBREWS 12:2 ESV

The LORD loves righteousness and justice;
the earth is full of his unfailing love.

PSALM 33:5

You will show me the path of life; in Your
presence is fullness of joy; at Your right
hand are pleasures forevermore.

PSALM 16:11 NKJV

My loving Lord,

I delight in hearing You say to me, *"I have loved you with an everlasting Love."* I confess that I cannot comprehend Your constancy because My mind is ever so human. My emotions flicker and falter in the face of varying circumstances, and it's easy for me to project my fickle feelings onto You. This keeps me from benefiting fully from *Your unfailing Love.*

Please teach me how to look beyond the flux of circumstances and find You gazing lovingly back at me. Such awareness of Your Presence strengthens me—helping me become more receptive and responsive to Your Love. I'm so grateful that *You are the same yesterday, today, and forever*! I want to open up to You more fully—letting Your Love flow into me continually. My need for You is as constant as the endless outflow of Your Love to me.

In Your steadfast Name, Jesus, Amen.

The Lord appeared to us in the past, saying: "I have loved you with an everlasting love; I have drawn you with loving-kindness."

JEREMIAH 31:3

In your unfailing love you will lead the people you have redeemed. In your strength you will guide them to your holy dwelling.

EXODUS 15:13

Jesus Christ is the same yesterday, today, and forever.

HEBREWS 13:8 NKJV

Whenever you start to feel anxious, remind yourself that your security rests in Me alone, and I am totally trustworthy. You will never be in control of your life circumstances, but you can relax and trust in My control.

My great God,

I'm grateful that *Your compassions never fail; they are new every morning.* So I can begin each day confidently, knowing that Your vast reservoir of blessings is full to the brim! This knowledge helps me wait for You, entrusting my long-unanswered prayers into Your care and keeping. I trust that not even one of my petitions has slipped past You unnoticed. As I wait in Your Presence, help me to drink deeply from Your fountain of limitless Love and unfailing compassion. These divine provisions are freely available to me—and essential for my spiritual health.

Although many of my prayers are not yet answered, I find hope in *Your great faithfulness.* You keep *all* Your promises—in Your perfect way and Your perfect timing. You have promised to give me Peace that can displace the trouble and fear in my heart. If I become weary of waiting, please remind me that You also wait—*so that You may be gracious to me and have mercy on me.* Like wise parents do, You hold back until I am ready to receive the things You have lovingly prepared for me. As I spend time in Your Presence, I rejoice in the promise that *all those who wait for You are blessed.*

In Your gracious Name, Jesus, Amen.

His compassions never fail. They are new every morning; great is your faithfulness. I say to myself, "The Lord is my portion; therefore I will wait for him."

Lamentations 3:22–24

"Peace I leave with you; my peace I give you. I do not give to you as the world gives. Do not let your hearts be troubled and do not be afraid."

John 14:27

The Lord will wait, that He may be gracious to you; and . . . He will be exalted, that He may have mercy on you. For the Lord is a God of justice; blessed are all those who wait for Him.

Isaiah 30:18 nkjv

My strong Deliverer,

As I face the circumstances of this day, I need to *lean on You*. Everyone leans on *something*: physical strength, intelligence, beauty, wealth, achievements, family, friends. All of these are gifts from You, and I want to enjoy Your blessings gratefully. But I've learned that depending on any of these things is risky—every single one of them can let me down.

When I'm facing challenging circumstances and I'm feeling weak, I tend to obsess about how I'm going to make it through the day. This wastes a lot of time and energy; even worse, it distracts me from my relationship with You. Whenever this happens, please open my eyes so I can find You in the midst of my circumstances. Enable me to "see" You standing nearby, with Your strong arms extended to me—offering me Your help. Instead of pretending that I have it all together or that I'm stronger than I really am, I can lean hard on You. As I do, You *bear my burdens* and show me how to deal with my difficulties.

I rejoice in You, *my Strength*. And *I sing praises to You, my loving God*.

In Your splendid Name, Jesus, Amen.

Lean on, trust in, and be confident in the Lord
with all your heart and mind and do not rely
on your own insight or understanding.

PROVERBS 3:5 AMPC

Praise be to the Lord, to God our Savior,
who daily bears our burdens.

PSALM 68:19

O my Strength, I sing praise to you; you, O
God, are my fortress, my loving God.

PSALM 59:17

Supreme Savior,

I don't want to be weighed down by the clutter in my life—lots of little chores waiting to be done *sometime*, in no particular order. When I focus too much on these petty tasks, trying to get all of them out of the way, I discover that they are endless. They can eat up as much time as I devote to them!

Thank You for showing me that the remedy is to stop trying to do all my chores at once—and just focus on the ones I need to do today. Please help me choose the tasks You want me to accomplish this day, letting the rest of them slip into the background of my mind. This makes it possible for me to keep *You* in the forefront of my awareness.

My ultimate goal is living close to You—ready to respond to Your initiatives. I can communicate with You most freely when my mind is uncluttered and turned toward You. As I *seek Your Face* throughout this day, I ask for Your Presence to bring order to my thoughts and Peace into my entire being.

In Your redeeming Name, Jesus, Amen.

Commit to the Lord whatever you do,
and your plans will succeed.

PROVERBS 16:3

Lead me in Your truth and teach me, for You are the
God of my salvation; for You I wait all the day.

PSALM 25:5 NASB 1995

When You said, "Seek My face," my heart said
to You, "Your face, Lord, I will seek."

PSALM 27:8 NKJV

You will keep him in perfect peace, whose mind
is stayed on You, because he trusts in You.

ISAIAH 26:3 NKJV

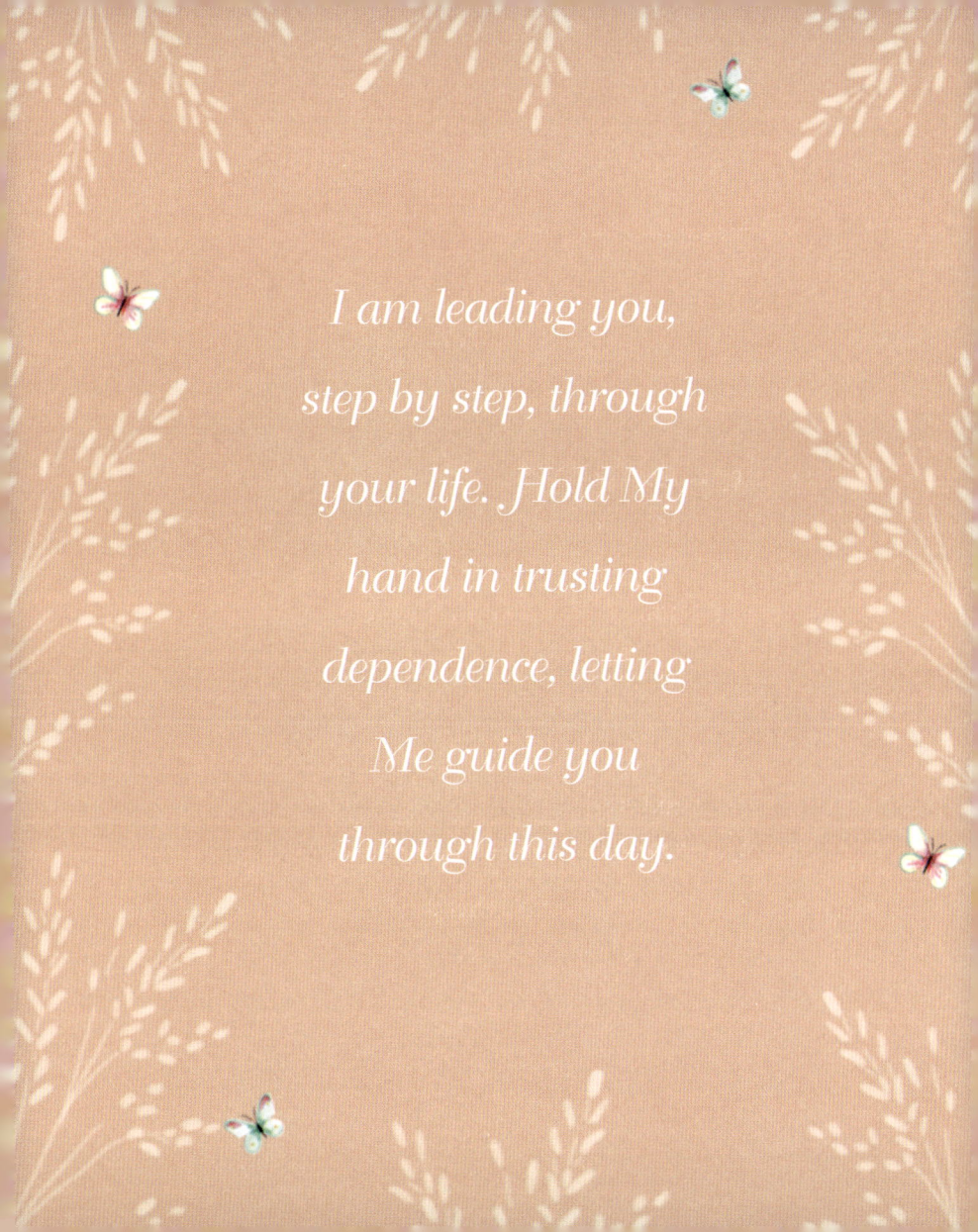

I am leading you, step by step, through your life. Hold My hand in trusting dependence, letting Me guide you through this day.

Merciful God,

Please help me to linger in gratitude. This is a most delightful place—where the Joy of Your Presence shines warmly upon me.

Often I pray fervently for something and wait hopefully for the answer. If You grant my request, I respond joyfully and thankfully. But my tendency is to move on rather quickly to seeking the next thing. Instead of experiencing only a short-lived burst of gratitude, I want to remain in an attitude of thankful Joy—letting my gratefulness flow freely into the future. I need to train myself to remember Your gracious response to my request. One way is to tell others about the blessing I've received from You, starting with my own family. Another way is to write down the prayer-answer someplace where I'll see it again and again.

Lord, teach me to *remember Your marvelous works* with thankfulness. You've been showing me that gratefulness blesses me doubly—with happy memories of answered prayer and with the delight of sharing Joy with You!

In Your joyful Name, Jesus, Amen.

Let us come before His presence with thanksgiving;
let us shout joyfully to Him with psalms.

PSALM 95:2 NKJV

Thanks be to God! He gives us the victory
through our Lord Jesus Christ.

1 CORINTHIANS 15:57

Remember His marvelous works which He has done,
His wonders, and the judgments of His mouth.

1 CHRONICLES 16:12 NKJV

ALL-KNOWING GOD,

I delight in the truth that *I am fully known*! You know absolutely everything about me, yet You love me with perfect, *unfailing Love*. I've spent many years searching for greater self-understanding and self-acceptance. Underlying this search is the desire to find someone who truly understands me and accepts me as I am. I've discovered that *You* are the Someone who can satisfy my deep-seated longing. In my relationship with You, I become more completely who I really am.

Help me to be increasingly real with You—dropping all pretenses and opening up fully to You. *Search me, O God, and know my heart; try me, and know my anxious thoughts.* In the Light of Your holy gaze, I can see many things I need to change. But I know You are with me in my efforts, so I won't despair. Instead, I'll rest in Your Presence, receiving Your Love that flows freely into me through my openness to You. As I take time to soak in this powerful Love, it fills up my empty spaces and overflows into joyous worship. I rejoice that I am perfectly known and forever loved!

IN YOUR LOVING NAME, JESUS, AMEN.

For now we see indistinctly, as in a mirror, but then face to face. Now I know in part, but then I will know fully, as I am fully known.

1 Corinthians 13:12 hcsb

The Lord delights in those who fear him, who put their hope in his unfailing love.

Psalm 147:11

Search me, God, and know my heart; try me and know my anxious thoughts; . . . and lead me in the everlasting way.

Psalm 139:23–24 nasb 1995

Holy Lord,

I love to *worship You in the beauty of holiness*. The beauty of Your creation reflects some of who You are, and it delights me! You are working Your ways in me: the divine Artist creating loveliness in my inner being. You've been clearing out the debris and clutter within me, making room for Your Spirit to take full residence. Help me to collaborate with You in this effort—being willing to let go of anything You choose to take away. You know exactly what I need, and You have promised to provide all of that—abundantly!

I don't want my sense of security to rest in my possessions, a peaceful home, or in things going my way. You are training me to depend on You alone, finding fulfillment in Your loving Presence. This involves being satisfied with much or with little of the world's goods, accepting *either* as Your will for me. Instead of grasping and controlling, I'm learning to release and receive. To cultivate this receptive stance, I need to trust You more—in any and every situation.

In Your beautiful Name, Jesus, Amen.

Give unto the Lord the glory due to His name;
worship the Lord in the beauty of holiness.

PSALM 29:2 NKJV

One thing I ask of the Lord, this is what I seek:
that I may dwell in the house of the Lord all
the days of my life, to gaze upon the beauty of
the Lord and to seek him in his temple.

PSALM 27:4

My God will supply all your needs according
to His riches in glory in Christ Jesus.

PHILIPPIANS 4:19 NASB 1995

The work I am doing in you is hidden at first. But eventually blossoms will burst forth, and abundant fruit will be born. Stay on the path of Life with Me. Trust Me wholeheartedly, letting My Spirit fill you with Joy and Peace.

Faithful God,

Morning by morning You awaken me and open my understanding to Your will. Thank You for always being mindful of me. It's comforting to know that You never sleep, so You're able to watch over me while I am sleeping. Then, *when I wake up, You are still with me.* As I become increasingly aware of Your Presence, You help me become more alert—combing out the tangles in my sleepy thoughts. I respond to Your Love-call by *drawing near to You.* I love to spend time enjoying Your Presence and nourishing my soul with Your Word.

I've found that time devoted to You blesses and strengthens me immensely. You open my understanding to Your Word—enabling me to comprehend Scripture better and apply it to my life. Please help me discern Your will clearly as I make plans for this day. When I walk alongside You, seeking to do Your will, You empower me to handle whatever comes my way.

Lord, teach me how to *trust in You at all times*—in all circumstances.

In Your trustworthy Name, Jesus, Amen.

Morning by morning [the Lord God] wakens me
and opens my understanding to his will.

ISAIAH 50:4 TLB

How precious are your thoughts about me, O
God. . . . When I wake up, you are still with me!

PSALM 139:17–18 NLT

Draw near to God and He will draw near to you.

JAMES 4:8 NKJV

Trust in him at all times, O people; pour out
your hearts to him, for God is our refuge.

PSALM 62:8

Gentle Jesus,

Sometimes I need Your help even to ask for help. As I try to do several things at once, I find myself moving faster and faster—interrupting one thing to do another. If my phone rings at such a time, my stress level rises even higher. Only when I *stop* everything, take a few deep breaths, and whisper Your Name do I begin to calm down. Then I can acknowledge my need for You to guide me through the day. You have promised to *lead me in paths of righteousness for Your Name's sake.*

When I'm preparing to do something challenging, I usually take time to ask for Your help. But when I do everyday tasks, I tend to dive in unassisted—acting as if I can handle these matters alone. Yet it's so much better to approach *everything* in humble dependence on You. Whenever I'm feeling tempted to just dive in, I need to stop and turn to You—asking You to show me the way forward. As I wait in Your loving Presence, I delight in hearing You speak these words of assurance: *"I will guide you along the best pathway for your life."*

In Your reassuring Name, Amen.

He restores my soul. He leads me in paths
of righteousness for his name's sake.

PSALM 23:3 ESV

God did this so that men would seek him and
perhaps reach out for him and find him, though
he is not far from each one of us. "For in him
we live and move and have our being."

ACTS 17:27–28

The LORD says, "I will guide you along the best pathway
for your life. I will advise and watch over you."

PSALM 32:8 NLT

Compassionate God,

How comforting it is to know that *You broaden the path beneath me so that my ankles do not turn*. Because You are in control, I don't need to worry about what will happen or wonder if I'll be able to cope. I realize that only *You* know what my future really holds—and You're the only One who fully understands what I'm capable of. Moreover, You can alter my circumstances at any time—gradually or dramatically. In fact, You can even widen the path I'm walking on right now.

Help me to really grasp how intricately involved You are in every aspect of my life. You're always taking care of me—tweaking circumstances to protect me and the ones I love from unnecessary hardship. Your Word says *You are a shield for all who take refuge in You*. I'm learning that my role in our adventurous journey is to trust You, stay in communication with You, and walk with You in steps of joyful dependence.

I know You don't remove all adversity from my life, but I'm thankful that You go before me and widen my pathway. This is one of the many ways You *bless me and keep me* safe.

In Your blessed Name, Jesus, Amen.

You broaden the path beneath me, so
that my ankles do not turn.

PSALM 18:36

As for God, his way is perfect: The LORD's word is flawless. He is a shield for all who take refuge in him.

PSALM 18:30

"The LORD bless you and keep you; the LORD make His face shine upon you, and be gracious to you; the LORD lift up His countenance upon you, and give you peace."

NUMBERS 6:24–26 NKJV

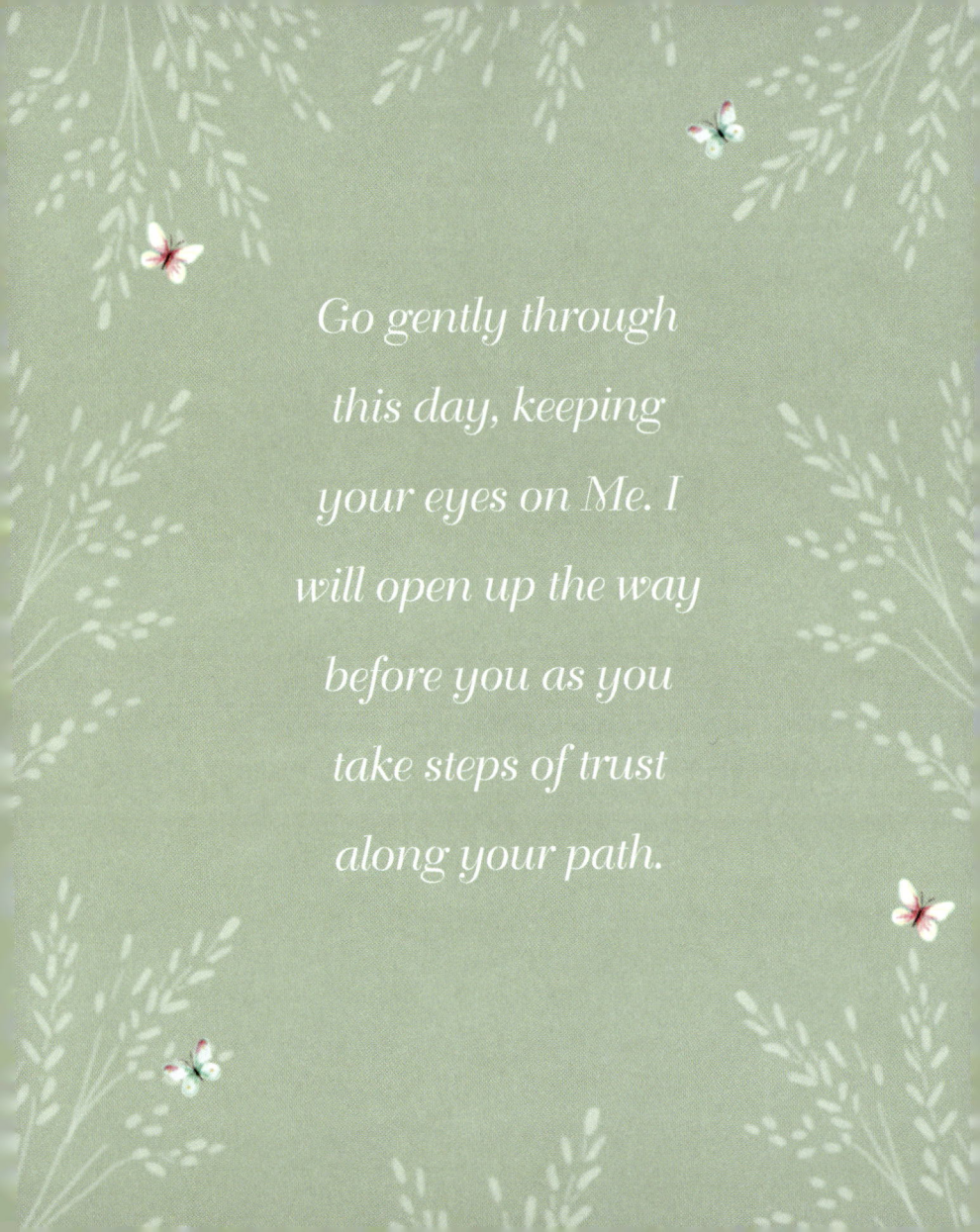

Go gently through this day, keeping your eyes on Me. I will open up the way before you as you take steps of trust along your path.

My ardent Lord,

Your Love chases after me every day of my life! So I'll look for signs of Your loving Presence as I go through this day. You disclose Yourself to me in a variety of ways—words of Scripture just when I need them, helpful words spoken through other people, "coincidences" orchestrated by Your Spirit, nature's beauty, and so on. Your Love for me is not passive. It actively chases after me and leaps into my life! Please open the eyes of my heart so I can "see" You blessing me in myriad ways—both small and great.

I want to not only receive Your bountiful blessings but also take careful note of them—treasuring them and *pondering them in my heart* as Your mother did, Jesus. I'm thankful for the countless ways You show up in my life. I like to write down some of these blessings so I can enjoy them again and again. These signs of Your Presence strengthen me and prepare me for whatever difficulties I'll encounter on the road ahead. Help me to remember that nothing can separate me from Your Love!

In Your conquering Name, Jesus, Amen.

Your beauty and love chase after me
every day of my life. I'm back home in the
house of God for the rest of my life.

Psalm 23:6 msg

Your word I have hidden in my heart,
that I might not sin against You.

Psalm 119:11 nkjv

Mary treasured up all these things and
pondered them in her heart.

Luke 2:19

Precious Jesus,

You are my Treasure! You're immeasurably more valuable than anything I can see, hear, or touch. *Knowing You* is *the Prize* above every other prize.

Earthly treasures are often hoarded, worried over, or hidden for safekeeping. But the riches I have in You can never be lost or stolen or damaged. In fact, I've found that as I share You freely with others, I gain even *more* of You. Since You are infinite, there will always be more of You for me to discover—and to love.

My world often feels fragmented, with countless things—both small and large—vying for my attention. So much "stuff" keeps getting in the way of my desire to spend time enjoying Your Presence. I admit that being *worried and bothered about many things* comes naturally to me. But Your Word assures me that *only one thing is necessary.* When I make You that *one thing,* I choose *what will not be taken away from me.*

Help me to rejoice in Your continual nearness—and to let my awareness of Your Presence put everything else in perspective. You are the Treasure that can brighten all my moments!

In Your priceless Name, Amen.

I press on toward the goal to win the prize for which
God has called me heavenward in Christ Jesus.

Philippians 3:14

"Do not store up for yourselves treasures
on earth, where moth and rust destroy, and
where thieves break in and steal."

Matthew 6:19

[Jesus] said to her, "Martha, Martha, you are worried
and distracted by and bothered about so many things;
but only one thing is necessary, for Mary has chosen the
good part, which shall not be taken away from her."

Luke 10:41–42 nasb 1995

Dearest Jesus,

How wonderful it is to know that You are taking care of me! When I'm spending time with You—enjoying the warmth and security of Your loving Presence—it's easier to trust that every detail of my life is under Your control. The Bible affirms that *everything fits into a plan for good, for those who love You and are called according to Your design and purpose.*

Because the world is in such an abnormal, fallen condition, it sometimes feels as if chance is governing the universe. Events seem to happen randomly, with little or no apparent meaning. But You've shown me that when I view the world this way, I'm overlooking a most important fact: the limitations of my understanding. Submerged beneath the surface of the visible world, there are mysteries too profound for me to fathom!

If I could actually *see* how close You are to me and my entire family—and how constantly You work on our behalf—I would never again doubt Your wonderful care. Your Word instructs me to *live by faith, not by sight.* Please help me to trust in Your mysterious, majestic Presence.

In Your magnificent Name, Amen.

We are assured and know that [God being a partner in their labor] all things work together and are [fitting into a plan] for good to and for those who love God and are called according to [His] design and purpose.

ROMANS 8:28 AMPC

[Job answered the Lord], "I have uttered what I did not understand, things too wonderful for me, which I did not know."

JOB 42:3 NKJV

Cast all your anxiety on him because he cares for you.

1 PETER 5:7

We live by faith, not by sight.

2 CORINTHIANS 5:7

EVER-NEAR JESUS,

You've been calling me to a life of constant communion with You. Part of the training involves living above my circumstances, even when I'm up to my neck in clutter and confusion. I yearn for a simplified lifestyle—with fewer interruptions to my communication with You. But you have been challenging me to relinquish the fantasy of an uncluttered world. I need to accept each day just as it comes to me—and *search for You* in the midst of it all.

I'm thankful that I can talk with You about every aspect of my day, including my feelings. Help me remember that my ultimate goal is *not* to control or fix everything around me; it's to keep communing with You. You've been showing me that a successful day is one in which I have stayed in touch with You—even if many things remain undone at the end of the day.

I must not let my to-do list become an idol directing my life. Instead, I can ask Your Spirit to guide me moment by moment. He will keep me close to You.

IN YOUR GUIDING NAME, AMEN.

Devote yourselves to prayer, being watchful and thankful.

COLOSSIANS 4:2

"You will seek Me and find Me when you search for Me with all your heart."

JEREMIAH 29:13 NASB 1995

Since we live by the Spirit, let us keep in step with the Spirit.

GALATIANS 5:25

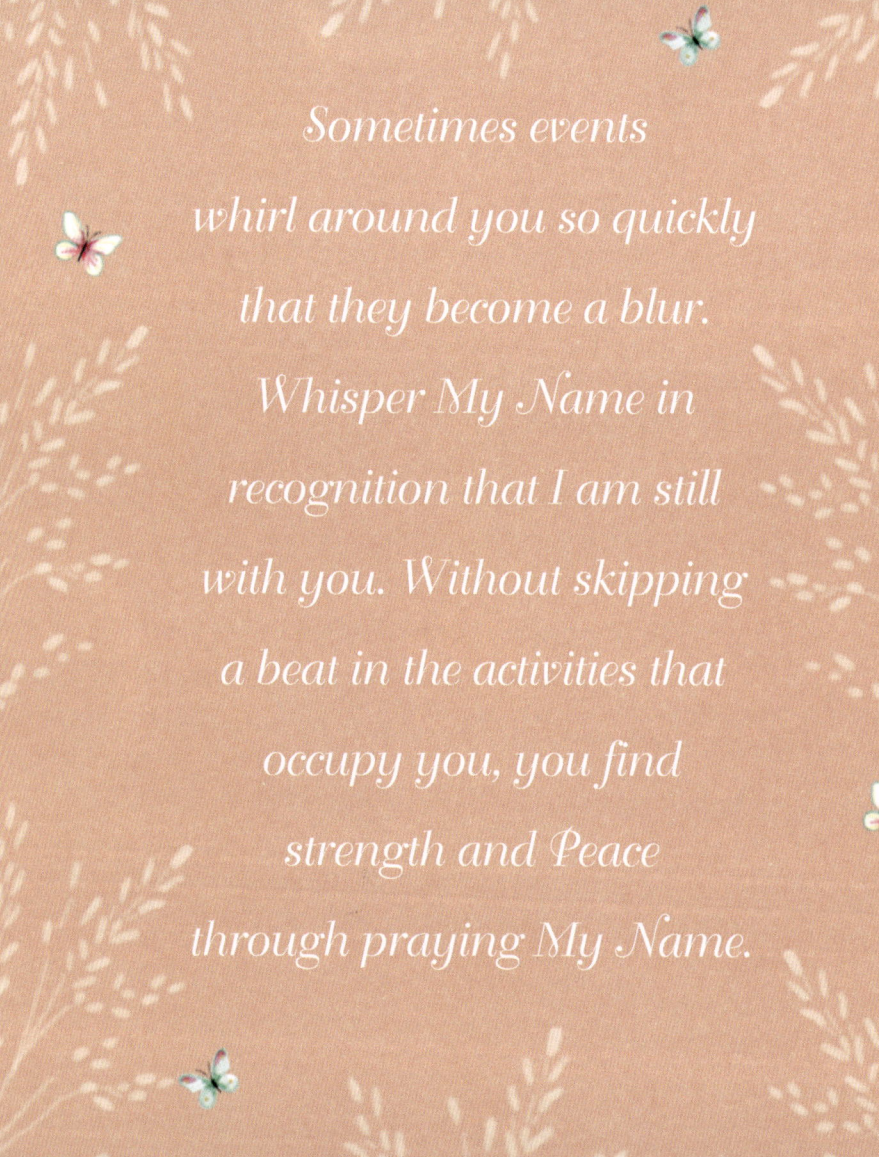

Sometimes events whirl around you so quickly that they become a blur. Whisper My Name in recognition that I am still with you. Without skipping a beat in the activities that occupy you, you find strength and Peace through praying My Name.

MY SAVIOR-GOD,

My soul clings to You; Your right hand upholds me. I know that You use difficult times to strengthen me spiritually. Just as gold is refined by fire, so *my faith* is refined by trials—to prove that it is genuine. As I cling to You in the midst of adversity, my faith grows stronger and I find comfort in You. When I endure trials in dependence on You, I gain confidence that I can cope with future hardships. More and more, I'm able to trust that You will always help me in my time of need.

In the middle of the night or in the midst of tough times, I remember that Your right hand is supporting me. This hand that holds me up is super-strong; there's no limit to how much support You can provide. So when I'm feeling overwhelmed, I won't give up. Instead, I'll *look to You and Your strength.*

Your hand is not only powerful but righteous. I love the assurance You give me in Your Word: *"Do not fear, for I am with you; do not be dismayed, for I am your God. I will strengthen you and help you; I will uphold you with My righteous right hand."*

IN YOUR POWERFUL NAME, JESUS, AMEN.

On my bed I remember you; I think of you through the watches of the night. . . . My soul clings to you; your right hand upholds me.

Psalm 63:6, 8

[All kinds of trials] have come so that your faith—of greater worth than gold, which perishes even though refined by fire—may be proved genuine.

1 Peter 1:7

"Do not fear, for I am with you; do not be dismayed, for I am your God. I will strengthen you and help you; I will uphold you with my righteous right hand."

Isaiah 41:10

My living Lord,

You are everything I could possibly need in a Savior-God, and *You live in me*! You fill me with radiant Life and Love. I want Your Life in me to overflow and impact other people. Please live through me and love through me as I interact with others, including my family. I ask that Your Love will grace my words and Your Light will reflect from my demeanor as I live in joyful dependence on You.

In this world I often feel insufficient, but I know *I am complete in You*, Lord. All that I need for my salvation and spiritual growth is found in You. Through *Your divine Power* I have everything necessary to persevere in my journey toward heaven. You bless me with intimate *knowledge of You*, and You invite me to open up and share with You at the deepest levels—both my struggles and my delights.

Your finished work on the cross provides deep rest for my soul, Lord Jesus. I'm so grateful that I am eternally secure in You—my living Savior and my forever-Friend.

In Your victorious Name, Jesus, Amen.

My old self has been crucified with Christ. It is
no longer I who live, but Christ lives in me.

GALATIANS 2:20 NLT

In [Christ] dwells all the fullness of the Godhead
bodily; and you are complete in Him, who is
the head of all principality and power.

COLOSSIANS 2:9–10 NKJV

His divine power has given us everything we need
for life and godliness through our knowledge of him
who called us by his own glory and goodness.

2 PETER 1:3

Glorious Lord,

I receive this day of life as a precious gift from You. I want to treat it as the treasure it is by *seeking Your Face* and prayerfully prioritizing. As I look at the day that stretches out before me, please help me discern what is most important. Show me how to set priorities according to Your will—using them to guide me as I go along my way. This will enable me to make good choices about the use of my time and energy. Then, when I reach the end of the day, I can feel at peace about the things I have done—and also about the things I have *not* done.

You've been teaching me to include You in everything I do. I've seen that even the briefest prayer is sufficient to invite You into my activities. By praying about everything, I acknowledge my continual need of You. I'm even learning to rejoice in my neediness—viewing it as a strong link to *Your glorious Presence*.

Although living in a dependent manner is countercultural, I've found that it's a blessed way to live—exulting in Your boundless sufficiency and *Your unfailing Love*.

In Your delightful Name, Jesus, Amen.

This is the day the Lord has made; we
will rejoice and be glad in it.

Psalm 118:24 nkjv

Glory in His holy name; let the heart of those
who seek the Lord be glad. Seek the Lord and
His strength; seek His face continually.

1 Chronicles 16:10–11 nasb 1995

May your unfailing love rest upon us, O
Lord, even as we put our hope in you.

Psalm 33:22

Bring Me the sacrifice of your time: a most precious commodity. In this action-addicted world, few of My children take time to sit quietly in My Presence. But for those who do, blessings flow like streams of living water.

Jesus, my splendid Companion,

I desire to walk with You in close, trusting Love-bonds of joyful dependence. The companionship You offer me sparkles with precious promises from the Bible: You love me with perfect, *everlasting Love*. You are always with me, guiding me through each moment of my life. You know everything about me, and You have already paid the penalty for all my sins. My inheritance—*kept in heaven for me—can never perish, spoil, or fade.*

You've shown me that dependence is an inescapable part of being human and of being a mom—You designed me to rely on You continually. Help me to view my constant need of You as a blessing. When I accept my dependent condition and stop striving to be self-sufficient, my awareness of Your loving Presence increases. Draw me closer to You, Lord, so I can enjoy Your marvelous Companionship.

I delight in Your invitation to walk with You in joyful dependence along the pathway of my life. And I love hearing You whisper: "Beloved, I am with you."

In Your marvelous Name, Amen.

The Lord has appeared of old to me, saying: "Yes,
I have loved you with an everlasting love."

JEREMIAH 31:3 NKJV

In him we have redemption through his blood,
the forgiveness of sins, in accordance with
the riches of God's grace that he lavished on
us with all wisdom and understanding.

EPHESIANS 1:7–8

In [God's] great mercy he has given us new birth into
a living hope through the resurrection of Jesus Christ
from the dead, and into an inheritance that can never
perish, spoil or fade—kept in heaven for you.

1 PETER 1:3–4

Compassionate Jesus,

I need to tell You about the things that have been weighing me down. I realize You already know all about them, but voicing them to You provides relief from the heavy load I've been carrying.

Whenever I'm feeling discouraged, it's essential for me to spend time *remembering You*. Thinking about who You are—*my Lord and my God*, my Savior and Shepherd, the Friend who *will never leave me*—lifts me up and brightens my perspective. I'm grateful that You are fully aware of every aspect of my life, including all my thoughts and feelings. Everything about me is important to You! As I relax in Your loving Presence, help me recall the many ways You've taken care of me, providing just what I need. I'll try to thank You for each blessing that comes to mind.

In the Light of Your Presence, I can see things more clearly and sort out what is important and what is not. As I linger with You, Your Face shines upon me—blessing, encouraging, and comforting me. *I will again praise You for the help of Your Presence.*

In Your mighty Name, Amen.

O my God, my soul is cast down within
me; therefore I will remember You.

PSALM 42:6 NKJV

Thomas responded to Him, "My Lord and my God!"

JOHN 20:28 HCSB

The LORD himself goes before you and will be with
you; he will never leave you nor forsake you.

DEUTERONOMY 31:8

Why are you in despair, O my soul? And why have
you become disturbed within me? Hope in God, for I
shall again praise Him for the help of His presence.

PSALM 42:5 NASB 1995

DELIGHTFUL LORD,

Your comforts delight my soul. This world presents me with a *multitude of anxieties*—too numerous for me to count. Everywhere I look, I see problems and trouble. In the midst of all this mess, I need to look to You over and over again. When I whisper Your Name, "Jesus," my awareness of Your Presence is renewed. My perspective changes dramatically as Your Presence lights up my mind—brightening my worldview. Your comforts delight my soul and soothe my troubled heart.

I realize I would never experience the pleasure of receiving comfort from You if the world were perfect. So instead of letting problems discourage me, I can choose to view them as reminders to seek *You*—Your Presence, Your Peace, Your Love. These invisible realities are always available to me, and they provide *Joy that no one will take away from me.*

I am blessed and encouraged by Your comforting invitation: *"Come to Me, all you who are weary and burdened, and I will give you rest."* Lord Jesus, I come to You.

IN YOUR WONDERFUL NAME, JESUS, AMEN.

In the multitude of my anxieties within
me, Your comforts delight my soul.

PSALM 94:19 NKJV

[Jesus said,] "A woman giving birth . . . has pain
because her time has come; but when her baby is
born she forgets the anguish because of her joy that
a child is born into the world. So with you: Now is
your time of grief, but I will see you again and you
will rejoice, and no one will take away your joy."

JOHN 16:21–22

"Come to me, all you who are weary and
burdened, and I will give you rest."

MATTHEW 11:28

Walk closely with Me each moment, listening for My directives and enjoying My Companionship. Refuse to let other voices tie you up in knots. My sheep know My voice and follow Me wherever I lead.

My Refuge,

You are worthy of all my confidence, all my trust! There are people and things that deserve *some* of my confidence and trust, but only You deserve *all* of it. In a world that seems increasingly unsafe and unpredictable, You are the Rock that provides a firm foundation for my life—*my Rock in whom I take refuge.*

Because You are my Refuge, my sense of security doesn't rest in my circumstances. My natural inclination is to strive to be in control, but You're training me to relax in *Your* sovereign control. You are *a well-proved help in trouble*, and You're always present with me. Please help me to face unwelcome changes and unnerving circumstances without fear.

Instead of letting anxious thoughts roam freely in my mind, I need to lasso them, voicing my trust in You. When I bring those captive thoughts into Your Presence, You subdue them and give me Your Peace. As Your Word assures me, *whoever trusts in You is kept safe.*

In Your strong Name, Jesus, Amen.

The Lord is my rock, my fortress and my deliverer;
my God is my rock, in whom I take refuge.

Psalm 18:2

God is our Refuge and Strength [mighty and
impenetrable to temptation], a very present
and well-proved help in trouble.

Psalm 46:1 ampc

Fear of man will prove to be a snare, but
whoever trusts in the Lord is kept safe.

Proverbs 29:25

BELOVED JESUS,

I want to be all Yours! I invite You to wean me from other dependencies. You have shown me that my security rests in You alone—not in other people, not in my circumstances.

Trying to depend only on You sometimes feels like walking on a tightrope. Yet I don't need to be afraid of falling because Your *everlasting arms* are a safety net underneath me.

Please help me to keep looking ahead to You, Jesus. I know that You're always before me, beckoning me on—one step at a time. As I spend quiet time with You, I can almost hear You whispering, "Follow Me, beloved."

Lord, *I am convinced that neither death nor life, neither angels nor demons, neither the present nor the future nor any powers, neither height nor depth, nor anything else in all creation, will be able to separate me from Your loving Presence!*

IN YOUR PRECIOUS NAME, AMEN.

The eternal God is your refuge, and
underneath are the everlasting arms.

DEUTERONOMY 33:27 NKJV

In his heart a man plans his course, but
the LORD determines his steps.

PROVERBS 16:9

I am convinced that neither death nor life, neither
angels nor demons, neither the present nor the future,
nor any powers, neither height nor depth, nor anything
else in all creation, will be able to separate us from
the love of God that is in Christ Jesus our Lord.

ROMANS 8:38–39

FAITHFUL GOD,

Help me to *learn the secret of being content in any and every situation*. I realize that contentment-training is a challenging process—learned through enduring a wide range of difficulties. I thought I was fairly advanced in this training, but then the circumstances of my life got harder. On some days I'm able to cope fairly well with all the stress. On other days I just want out! Please teach me how to handle the "other days."

I am so grateful that I can *pour out my heart to You*—acknowledging how frustrated and upset I'm feeling. Just releasing those pent-up feelings in Your Presence does me a world of good. Knowing that You completely understand me *and* my circumstances encourages me even more.

Lord, would You please deepen my awareness of Your continual Presence with me? I know I need to stay in communication with You—talking with You, bathing my mind and heart in scriptures that speak to my situation. And singing praises to You lifts my spirits like nothing else! *It is good to sing praises to Your Name—declaring Your lovingkindness in the morning and Your faithfulness every night.*

IN YOUR LOVING NAME, JESUS, AMEN.

I have learned the secret of being content
in any and every situation.

PHILIPPIANS 4:12

Trust in him at all times, O people; pour out
your hearts to him, for God is our refuge.

PSALM 62:8

It is good to give thanks to the LORD, and to sing praises to
Your name, O Most High; to declare Your lovingkindness
in the morning, and Your faithfulness every night.

PSALM 92:1–2 NKJV

My loving Lord,

You are good and Your Love endures forever! The best response to this promise is *giving thanks to You and praising Your Name.* Please help me to do this more consistently.

Lord, I'm so grateful for Your goodness! If there were even a speck of badness in You, I would be in uttermost peril. But Your absolute goodness guarantees that You always do what is best. I say this as a statement of faith because my family and I live in such a fractured, fallen world. So it's essential that I walk by faith, *trusting in You* as I journey through the wilderness of this world.

Giving You thanks and praising Your Name are ways I find strength for my journey. Thanksgiving and worship lift my perspective from my worries and woes to the glorious Treasure I have in You, Jesus. Thankfulness puts me in proper alignment with You—my Creator and Savior. Worship deepens and enriches my intimacy with You. I rejoice that the more I praise You, the closer to You I grow. As I spend time worshiping You, I delight in remembering that *Your steadfast Love endures forever*!

In Your faithful Name, Jesus, Amen.

Enter his gates with thanksgiving and his courts with praise; give thanks to him and praise his name. For the Lord is good and his love endures forever; his faithfulness continues through all generations.

Psalm 100:4–5

As for me, I trust in You, O Lord;
I say, "You are my God."

Psalm 31:14 nkjv

Give thanks to the Lord, for he is good, for his steadfast love endures forever.

Psalm 136:1 esv

Do not fear My will, for through it I accomplish what is best for you. Take a deep breath and dive into the depths of absolute trust in Me.

MY GREAT GOD,

I don't want to let any set of circumstances intimidate me. Please keep reminding me that the more challenging my day is, the more of Your Power You provide.

I used to think that You empower me equally each day, but I've learned that this is not true. Still, my tendency upon awakening each morning is to assess the difficulties ahead of me—measuring them against my average strength. I realize these worry-thoughts are just an exercise in unreality, and I long to break free from them!

Lord, You know what each of my days will contain, and I can trust You to empower me accordingly. You've been showing me that the degree to which You strengthen me on a given day is based mainly on two variables: the difficulty of my circumstances and my willingness to depend on You as I'm dealing with those challenges.

Help me view difficult days as opportunities to receive more of Your Power than usual. Instead of panicking during tough times, I can look to You for all I need. Thank You for Your reassuring words: *"As your days, so shall your strength be."*

IN YOUR STRONG NAME, JESUS, AMEN.

He said to me, "My grace is sufficient for you, for
my power is made perfect in weakness." Therefore I
will boast all the more gladly about my weaknesses,
so that Christ's power may rest on me.

2 Corinthians 12:9

Seek the Lord and His strength; seek His face continually.

Psalm 105:4 nasb 1995

Your sandals shall be iron and bronze; as
your days, so shall your strength be.

Deuteronomy 33:25 nkjv

FAITHFUL GOD,

I need to stop trying to work things out before their times have come. Help me to accept the limitations of living one day at a time. When something comes to my attention, I can pause and ask You whether it's part of today's agenda for me. If it is not, I can just release it into Your care and keeping—and move on to today's responsibilities. I've found that when I follow this practice, there's a beautiful simplicity about my life: *a time for everything*, and everything in its time.

You have promised many blessings to *those who wait for You: new strength*, resurgence of hope, awareness of Your continual Presence. Waiting for You enables me to glorify You by living in deep dependence on You, ready to do Your will.

I've discovered that living close to You makes my life less complicated and cluttered. Though the world around me is messy and confusing, I rejoice that *You have overcome the world*. Thank You for *telling me these things, so that in You I may have Peace*.

IN YOUR WONDERFUL NAME, JESUS, AMEN.

There is a time for everything, and a season
for every activity under heaven.

ECCLESIASTES 3:1

Those who wait for the LORD will gain new strength; they
will mount up with wings like eagles; they will run and
not get tired, they will walk and not become weary.

ISAIAH 40:31 NASB 1995

"I have told you these things, so that in me you may
have peace. In this world you will have trouble.
But take heart! I have overcome the world."

JOHN 16:33

My Savior-God,

When many things seem to be going wrong and my life feels increasingly out of control, help me to trust You and thank You. These are supernatural responses that can lift me above my circumstances. If I do what comes *naturally* in the face of difficulties, I tend to fall prey to negativism.

Even a few complaints can darken my perspective and set me on a downward spiral. With this negative attitude controlling me, complaints flow more and more readily from my mouth. Each one moves me further down the slippery slope, and the lower I go, the faster I slide. But it's always possible to apply the brakes by crying out to You in Your Name—affirming my trust in You and *giving thanks for everything.* Though this feels unnatural, I've learned that if I persist in these responses, I will gradually move back up the slope.

Once I've recovered all my lost ground, I can face my circumstances from a humble perspective. If I choose supernatural responses this time—trusting and thanking You—*Your Peace that surpasses understanding will guard my heart and my mind.*

In Your unsurpassed Name, Jesus, Amen.

I trust in your unfailing love; my heart
rejoices in your salvation.

Psalm 13:5

Give thanks for everything to God the Father
in the name of our Lord Jesus Christ.

Ephesians 5:20 nlt

Do not be anxious about anything, but in everything
by prayer and supplication with thanksgiving let your
requests be made known to God. And the peace of
God, which surpasses all understanding, will guard
your hearts and your minds in Christ Jesus.

Philippians 4:6–7 esv

I want you to learn the art of giving thanks in all circumstances. See how many times you can thank Me daily; this will awaken your awareness to a multitude of blessings. It will also cushion the impact of trials when they come against you.

Glorious Jesus,

You are the firm foundation on which I can dance and sing and celebrate Your glorious Presence! I receive this precious gift as Your high and holy calling for me. You've shown me that glorifying and enjoying You is vastly more important than maintaining a tidy, structured life. Still, my natural tendency is to pour my energy into trying to keep everything under control. Help me relinquish this striving to be in control—recognizing that it's both an impossible task and an affront to *Your faithfulness*.

I realize that You guide each of Your children individually. That's why listening to You—through Scripture and prayer—is essential for me to find the way forward. Please prepare me for the day that awaits me and point me in the right direction. Because You are with me continually, I don't have to be intimidated by fear. Though it stalks me, I know it can't harm me as long as I cling to Your hand. Instead of being fearful, I want to walk trustingly with You along my pathway--enjoying Peace in Your Presence.

In Your high and holy Name, Amen.

Let all who take refuge in You be glad, let them ever sing for joy; and may You shelter them, that those who love Your name may exult in You.

PSALM 5:11 NASB 1995

Because of the LORD's faithful love we do not perish, for His mercies never end. They are new every morning; great is Your faithfulness!

LAMENTATIONS 3:22–23 HCSB

To him who is able to keep you from falling and to present you before his glorious presence without fault and with great joy—to the only God our Savior be glory, majesty, power and authority, through Jesus Christ our Lord.

JUDE 24–25

My Shepherd,

Please help me to relax and enjoy this day. It's easy for me to get so focused on my goals that I push myself too hard—and neglect my need for rest. I tend to judge myself on the basis of how much I'm accomplishing. I know it's important for me to use the opportunities and abilities You provide, but I want to learn to accept myself as much when I'm relaxing as when I'm achieving.

Teach me how to rest deeply in the truth that I'm a beloved child of God, *saved by grace through faith* in You. I know *this* is my ultimate—and foundational—identity. I rejoice that I've been adopted into Your royal family forever! Instead of striving and straining, I need to stay mindful of who I really am.

I've found that I'm more effective in Your kingdom when I'm comfortable enough in my true identity to balance family, work, and rest. With a refreshed mind, I'm able to think more clearly and biblically. And a *restored soul* enables me to be more loving with other people.

Lord, I long to spend time relaxing in Your Presence today—enjoying the *fresh green pastures* and *still, restful waters* You provide.

In Your refreshing Name, Jesus, Amen.

By grace you have been saved through faith.
And this is not your own doing; it is the gift
of God . . . so that no one can boast.

EPHESIANS 2:8–9 ESV

Rest in God alone, my soul, for my
hope comes from Him.

PSALM 62:5 HCSB

He restores my soul; He leads me in the paths
of righteousness for His name's sake.

PSALM 23:3 NKJV

He makes me lie down in [fresh, tender] green pastures;
He leads me beside the still and restful waters.

PSALM 23:2 AMPC

Cherished Jesus,

My life is a precious gift from You. So I open my hands and heart to receive this day of life gratefully. I love relating to You as my Friend and Savior, but I need to remember that You are also my Creator-God. The Bible proclaims that *all things were created by You and for You.* As I go through this day that You've gifted to me, help me to find signs of Your abiding Presence along the way. And please attune my heart to hear You whisper: *"I am with you and will watch over you wherever you go."*

On bright, joyful days, I can speak to You about the pleasures You provide. Thanking You for them makes my Joy expand exponentially! On difficult days, I can grasp Your hand in trusting dependence—clinging to Your promise that *You will help me.*

My physical life is an amazing gift, but my spiritual life is a treasure of *infinite* value. Because I belong to You, I will live with You forever—enjoying a glorified body that will never get sick or grow tired. Thank You for the priceless gift of salvation by grace through faith!

In Your saving Name, Amen.

Things in heaven and on earth, visible and invisible, whether thrones or powers or rulers or authorities; all things were created by him and for him.

COLOSSIANS 1:16

"I am with you and will watch over you wherever you go, and I will bring you back to this land."

GENESIS 28:15

"I am the Lord, your God, who takes hold of your right hand and says to you, Do not fear; I will help you."

ISAIAH 41:13

O Most High,

When I declare the wonders of Your loving Presence, I find strength and encouragement in You. This glorious blessing flows into me even more fully when I speak the words out loud. As I'm proclaiming Your Love, help me to *rejoice with Joy that's inexpressible and filled with Glory*!

Your amazing Love is sacrificial, unfailing, priceless, and boundless—*reaching to the heavens*. It shines so brightly that it can carry me through all my days, even the darkest ones.

When I get to the end of each day, it's time to declare Your faithfulness that *reaches to the skies*. As I look back over the day, I can see how skillfully You guided me and opened up the way before me. The more difficulties I encountered, the more You enabled, empowered, and equipped me to overcome the obstacles.

It is good to give voice to Your great faithfulness, especially at night, so that I can *lie down and sleep in peace*.

In Your peaceful Name, Jesus, Amen.

Though you have not seen him, you love him. Though you do not now see him, you believe in him and rejoice with joy that is inexpressible and filled with glory.

1 PETER 1:8 ESV

Your love, O LORD, reaches to the heavens,
your faithfulness to the skies.

PSALM 36:5

I will lie down and sleep in peace, for you alone, LORD, make me dwell in safety.

PSALM 4:8

This is essentially an act of faith: believing that I love you with boundless, everlasting Love. The art of receiving is also a discipline: training your mind to trust Me, coming close to Me with confidence.

Wonderful Lord,

This is a time of abundance in my life—*my cup overflows* with blessings. After plodding uphill for many weeks, now I feel as if I'm traipsing through lush meadows drenched in sunshine. Help me enjoy this time of ease and refreshment to the max. Thank You for providing it for me!

While I love giving gifts, I admit that sometimes I hesitate to receive Your good gifts with open hands. Feelings of false guilt creep in, telling me I shouldn't accept these gifts since I don't deserve to be so richly blessed. But I realize this is fuzzy thinking, because no one *deserves* anything good from You. How I rejoice that Your kingdom is *not* about earning and deserving! It's about believing and receiving.

Instead of balking at accepting Your gracious gifts, I want to receive all Your blessings with a grateful heart. Then Your pleasure in giving and my pleasure in receiving can flow together joyously.

In Your generous Name, Jesus, Amen.

You prepare a table before me in the presence of my enemies; You anoint my head with oil; my cup overflows.

PSALM 23:5 HCSB

"Ask and it will be given to you; seek and you will find; knock and the door will be opened to you. For everyone who asks receives; he who seeks finds; and to him who knocks, the door will be opened."

LUKE 11:9–10

He who did not spare his own Son, but gave him up for us all—how will he not also, along with him, graciously give us all things?

ROMANS 8:32

BLESSED JESUS,

Please help me not to be afraid of being happy. Sometimes anxiety intrudes upon my carefree moments. I start wondering whether there are things I should be doing or plans I should be making. My underlying feeling is that it really isn't safe to let down my guard and simply savor the moment. But I know this kind of thinking is all wrong. Because I belong to You, I can expect to experience a measure of happiness—even in this deeply broken world.

The Bible teaches me to *cease striving*—let go, relax— and *know that You are God*. I used to think I needed to have all my ducks in a row before I could relax and enjoy Your Presence. But then I considered the overall context of this command: *though the earth give way and the mountains fall into the heart of the sea*. The psalmist who penned these words was describing a terrifying catastrophe! So I don't have to wait until all my problems are solved before daring to be happy. This very moment is the perfect time to *delight myself in You*.

Lord Jesus, I choose to enjoy You here and now!

IN YOUR JOYFUL NAME, AMEN.

Happy are the people whose God is the Lord!

Psalm 144:15 nkjv

"Cease striving and know that I am God; I will be exalted among the nations, I will be exalted in the earth."

Psalm 46:10 nasb 1995

God is our refuge and strength. . . . Therefore we will not fear, though the earth give way and the mountains fall into the heart of the sea.

Psalm 46:1–2

Mighty God,

You empower me—*infusing inner strength into me* so that I'm *ready for anything and equal to anything.* Please help me remember that this inner strength comes *through You,* Jesus, through my connection with You. It comes to me as I need it—as I take trusting steps of dependence, keeping my eyes on You. This promise is a powerful antidote to fear—especially my fear of being overwhelmed by the circumstances I see looming ahead. No matter how daunting they may look, I can trust that I am indeed ready for anything You bring into my life.

I'm thankful that You carefully control everything that happens. Moreover, You are constantly protecting me and the ones I love from both known and unknown dangers. And You provide strength, just when I need it, for coping with challenging circumstances.

You've been teaching me that many of the future things I anxiously anticipate will not actually reach me. Your promise is for the things I face in the present—and it is sufficient. So when I'm feeling the strain of an uphill journey, I need to stop and tell myself the truth: *"I have strength for all things in Christ Who empowers me!"*

In Your strong Name, Jesus, Amen.

I have strength for all things in Christ Who empowers me [I am ready for anything and equal to anything through Him Who infuses inner strength into me; I am self-sufficient in Christ's sufficiency].

PHILIPPIANS 4:13 AMPC

"Abide in Me, and I in you. As the branch cannot bear fruit of itself, unless it abides in the vine, neither can you, unless you abide in Me."

JOHN 15:4 NKJV

"Do not worry about tomorrow, for tomorrow will worry about itself. Each day has enough trouble of its own."

MATTHEW 6:34

Awareness of your inadequacy is not something you should try to evade. It is precisely where I want you—the best place to encounter Me in My Glory and Power.

Gracious God,

As I journey with You today, please help me to thank You all through the day. This practice makes it more feasible for me to *pray without ceasing*, as the apostle Paul taught. I long to be able to pray continually, and thanking You in every situation facilitates this pursuit. My thankful prayers provide a solid foundation on which I can build all my other prayers. Moreover, it's so much easier for me to communicate freely with You when I have a grateful attitude.

If I keep my mind occupied with thanking You, I'm less likely to fall into hurtful patterns of worrying or complaining. I've seen that when I practice thankfulness consistently, negative thought patterns gradually grow weaker and weaker.

A grateful heart opens up the way for me to *draw near to You*. And Your glorious Presence fills me with *Joy and Peace*.

In Your joyous Name, Jesus, Amen.

Rejoice always, pray without ceasing, give thanks in all circumstances; for this is the will of God in Christ Jesus for you.

1 THESSALONIANS 5:16–18 ESV

Draw near to God and He will draw near to you. Cleanse your hands, you sinners; and purify your hearts, you double-minded.

JAMES 4:8 NKJV

May the God of hope fill you with all joy and peace as you trust in him, so that you may overflow with hope by the power of the Holy Spirit.

ROMANS 15:13

MIGHTY GOD,

I'm thankful that *You are able to do immeasurably more than all I ask or imagine*. I like to think big when I pray, but I know that You always think much bigger! You are continually at work in my life, even when I can see nothing happening.

I tend to feel stuck in situations I'd like to change because I can see only the present moment. But *You* look at the big picture—all the moments of my life—and You are doing far more than I can comprehend.

Please help me stay in communication with You as I go through this day. I want to begin the day in joyful awareness of Your Presence—bringing You my praises and requests. This time of focusing my attention on You makes it easier to continue talking with You as I go about my activities and mundane tasks.

I've learned that the longer I wait to start communicating with You, the more effort it takes. So I like to come to You early, while the day is young and distractions are few. Sometimes I think I can't spare the time for this, but then I remember that I don't do my tasks alone. I work alongside the One *who can do more than I ask or imagine*!

IN YOUR GLORIOUS NAME, JESUS, AMEN.

Now to him who is able to do immeasurably more than all we ask or imagine, according to his power that is at work within us.

EPHESIANS 3:20

Jesus looked at them and said, "With man this is impossible, but with God all things are possible."

MATTHEW 19:26

In the morning, LORD, you hear my voice; in the morning I lay my requests before you and wait in expectation.

PSALM 5:3

My loving God,

Sometimes I hear You whispering in my heart: "Relax, My child. I'm in control." I like to let these words wash over me repeatedly, like soothing waves on a beautiful beach—assuring me of Your endless Love.

I confess that I waste a lot of time and energy trying to figure things out before their time has come. All the while, You are working to prepare the way before me. So I ask You to open my eyes to Your wonderful surprises—circumstances that only You could have orchestrated. Please keep reminding me that I am Your beloved. You are on my side and You want what is best for me.

Someone who is loved by a generous, powerful person can expect to receive an abundance of blessings. I rejoice that I am loved by *You,* the King of the universe, and *You have good plans for me.* As I look ahead into the unknown future, help me to relax in Your assurance of who I am—*the one You love.* Then I can go forward with confidence, clinging to Your hand. While You and I walk together along *the path of Life,* You fill my heart with Joy and my mind with Peace.

In Your beautiful Name, Jesus, Amen.

"I know the plans I have for you," declares the LORD, "plans to prosper you and not to harm you, plans to give you hope and a future."

JEREMIAH 29:11

About Benjamin he said: "Let the beloved of the LORD rest secure in him, for he shields him all day long, and the one the LORD loves rests between his shoulders."

DEUTERONOMY 33:12

You will show me the path of life; in Your presence is fullness of joy; at Your right hand are pleasures forevermore.

PSALM 16:11 NKJV

SOVEREIGN GOD,

You guide me in the way of wisdom and lead me along straight paths. Yet I sometimes feel so confused—struggling to find the right way forward. I've tried so many things, and I've been so hopeful at times. But my hope-filled paths have led to disappointment. I'm thankful that You fully understand how hard my journey has been. Even though I wish for easier circumstances, I believe that You can bring good out of every bit of my struggle.

Help me to walk in the way of wisdom—trusting You no matter what happens in my life. I know that steadfast trust in You is essential for finding and following the right path. As I go along my journey, I encounter many things that seem random or wrong. Yet I believe that You are fitting all of them into a comprehensive *plan for good*—Your Master Plan.

I realize that I can see only a very small piece of a massively big picture. From my limited vantage point, my parenting journey looks confusing, with puzzling twists and turns. But I'm learning to walk by faith—trusting that You are indeed *leading me along straight paths*.

IN YOUR GREAT, WISE NAME, JESUS, AMEN.

I guide you in the way of wisdom and
lead you along straight paths.

PROVERBS 4:11

We are assured and know that [God being a partner in their labor] all things work together and are [fitting into a plan] for good to and for those who love God and are called according to [His] design and purpose.

ROMANS 8:28 AMPC

A man's steps are directed by the LORD. How then can anyone understand his own way?

PROVERBS 20:24

Come to Me when you are weak and weary. Rest snugly in My everlasting arms. I do not despise your weakness, My child. Actually, it draws Me closer to you because weakness stirs up My compassion—My yearning to help. Accept yourself in your weariness, knowing that I understand how difficult your journey has been.

SPLENDID SAVIOR,

Your Word tells me: *If anything is excellent or praiseworthy, think about such things.* This sounds easy, but putting it into practice is really hard for me.

I've seen how countercultural it is to focus on admirable things. People who work in the media almost always shine their spotlights on negative news. They rarely bother to report good things that are happening—especially the many good things Your people are doing.

I admit that having a positive focus is not only countercultural but counter to my fallen nature. When Adam and Eve rebelled against You, *everything* was damaged by the Fall—including my mind. As a result, focusing on excellent, admirable things is not at all natural to me. It requires persistent effort, trying to make the right choice over and over again. Lord, please help me choose to look for what is good—daily, moment by moment—so that I may honor You *and* set a strong example for my children.

In spite of the massive problems in this world, there is much that is worthy of praise. I rejoice that You, the One who is the *most* praiseworthy, are *continually with me*—closer than my thoughts!

IN YOUR EXCELLENT, ADMIRABLE NAME, JESUS, AMEN.

Whatever is true, whatever is noble, whatever is right, whatever is pure, whatever is lovely, whatever is admirable—if anything is excellent or praiseworthy—think about such things.

PHILIPPIANS 4:8

Rejoice in the Lord always. I will say it again: Rejoice!

PHILIPPIANS 4:4

I am continually with You; You hold me by my right hand.

PSALM 73:23 NKJV

Dear Jesus,

I know that You are with me, so please help me not to be afraid. I love to hear You saying, *"Peace, be still!"* to my troubled heart. You have assured me that no matter what happens, *You will not leave me or forsake me.* When I let this assurance soak into my mind and heart, it fills me with confident trust.

The media relentlessly proclaims bad news: for breakfast, lunch, and dinner. I've found that a steady diet of its fare sickens me. Instead of focusing on fickle, ever-changing news, I choose to tune in to the living Word—*You,* the One who is always the same.

I want to let Scripture saturate my mind and heart so I can walk steadily along the path of Life with You. Although I don't know what will happen tomorrow, I can be absolutely sure of my ultimate destination. *You guide me with Your counsel, and afterward You will take me into Glory.* Hallelujah!

In Your magnificent Name, Amen.

Then He arose and rebuked the wind, and
said to the sea, "Peace, be still!" And the wind
ceased and there was a great calm.

MARK 4:39 NKJV

The LORD your God goes with you; he will
never leave you nor forsake you.

DEUTERONOMY 31:6 ESV

You guide me with your counsel, and
afterward you will take me into glory.

PSALM 73:24

Precious Jesus,

I've discovered that thanking You frequently not only awakens my heart to Your Presence but sharpens my mind. So when I'm feeling out of focus or out of touch with You, I need to make every effort to thank You for *something*. There is always an abundance of things to choose from: eternal gifts—such as salvation, grace, and faith—as well as ordinary, everyday blessings.

You've been training me to look back over the previous twenty-four hours and make note of all the good things You've provided, jotting down some of them in a journal. This discipline lifts my spirits and energizes me, enabling me to think more clearly.

The Bible teaches that *my enemy the devil prowls around like a roaring lion looking for someone to devour.* So it's very important for me to *be self-controlled and alert.* When I lose focus and let my thoughts drift, I'm much more vulnerable to the evil one's attacks. Please alert me whenever I'm in this vulnerable condition, and help me to drive away the enemy by thanking and praising You. This is warfare worship!

In Your praiseworthy Name, Amen.

The grace of God has appeared,
bringing salvation for all people.

TITUS 2:11 ESV

Be self-controlled and alert. Your enemy
the devil prowls around like a roaring
lion looking for someone to devour.

1 PETER 5:8

Thanks be to God for His indescribable gift!

2 CORINTHIANS 9:15 NKJV

Cultivate a thankful heart, for this glorifies Me and fills you with Joy.

Everlasting God,

Help me to worship You only—making You first and foremost in my life. The Bible teaches that You are *a jealous God* and that idolatry has always been the downfall of Your people. Current idols are more subtle than ancient ones because today's false gods are often secular. People, possessions, status, and wealth are some of the most popular idols these days.

You've been showing me that false gods never satisfy; instead, they stir up lust for more and more. When I seek *You* instead of the world's idols, I experience Your *Joy and Peace*. These priceless intangibles quench the thirst of my soul, providing deep satisfaction. The glitter of the world is tinny and temporal. The Light of Your Presence is brilliant and everlasting. I want to *walk in the Light* with You—becoming a beacon through whom others are drawn to You.

In Your priceless Name, Jesus, Amen.

Do not worship any other god, for the Lord, whose name is Jealous, is a jealous God.

Exodus 34:14

May the God of hope fill you with all joy and peace as you trust in him, so that you may overflow with hope by the power of the Holy Spirit.

Romans 15:13

If we walk in the light as He is in the light, we have fellowship with one another, and the blood of Jesus Christ His Son cleanses us from all sin.

1 John 1:7 nkjv

LORD JESUS,

I'm trying to trust that Your intentions for me are good even when they are radically different from what I'd hoped or expected. *You are Light; in You there is no darkness at all*. I will look for Your Light in my circumstances, for You are abundantly present in the moments of my life. I want to be open to You and all Your ways with me. Sometimes this requires relinquishing plans or dreams that are precious to me. At such times, I need to remember and wholeheartedly believe that *Your way is perfect*—no matter how hard it is.

You are a shield for all who take refuge in You. When I'm feeling disappointed or afraid, draw me closer to You, reminding me that You are my Refuge. I realize You don't shield me from absolutely everything. There are some trials You have prepared for me to handle. Thank You for giving me a significant part to play in this world—including the blessing and sacrifice of being "Mom." Please help me *lead the life You have assigned to me* in joyful dependence on You. Then *my soul will be satisfied as with the richest of foods; with singing lips my mouth will praise You*!

IN YOUR SUPREME NAME, AMEN.

God is Light, and in Him there is no darkness at all.

1 JOHN 1:5 NASB 1995

As for God, his way is perfect: The LORD's way is flawless. He is a shield for all who take refuge in him.

PSALM 18:30

Let each person lead the life that the Lord has assigned to him, and to which God has called him.

1 CORINTHIANS 7:17 ESV

My soul will be satisfied as with the richest of foods; with singing lips my mouth will praise you.

PSALM 63:5

Cherished Jesus,

Sometimes I feel frazzled—pulled this way and that by people and circumstances around me. At such times, I need to stop and turn to You, but instead I tend to drive myself to get more and more done. Even if I manage to calm my body, my mind continues to race—anticipating future problems and searching for solutions.

Help me to focus on the wondrous truth that *all the treasures of wisdom and knowledge are hidden in You*. Please remind me often, whispering to my heart: "Beloved, I am your Treasure. In Me you are complete."

When I prize You above all else, delighting in You as *my First Love*, I'm protected from feeling fragmented. You are the One who completes me, and You're training me to bring my thoughts back to You whenever they wander from Your Presence. Thank You for Your patient work in me, Lord.

Living near You, enjoying Your Presence, includes seeking to obey Your commands. I confess that I fail frequently, and I'm eternally grateful that *You have clothed me with garments of salvation—the robe of Your righteousness*!

In Your holy Name, Amen.

In [Christ] are hidden all the treasures
of wisdom and knowledge.

COLOSSIANS 2:3

"I have this against you, that you
have left your first love."

REVELATION 2:4 NKJV

I will greatly rejoice in the LORD; my soul shall
exult in my God, for he has clothed me with
the garments of salvation; he has covered
me with the robe of righteousness . . . as a
bride adorns herself with her jewels.

ISAIAH 61:10 ESV

You don't have to choose between staying close to Me and staying on course. Since I am the Way, staying close to Me is staying on course. As you focus your thoughts on Me, I will guide you carefully along today's journey.

GRACIOUS GOD,

You are so great, glorious, and compassionate that it's impossible to praise or thank You too much! *You inhabit the praises of Your people,* and I delight in drawing near You through worship. Sometimes my adoration is a spontaneous overflow of Joy—in response to rich blessings or radiant beauty. At other times my praise is more disciplined and measured—an act of my will. I'm grateful that You dwell in both types of praise.

I've discovered that thankfulness is a wonderful way to enjoy Your Presence. A grateful heart has plenty of room for You. When I thank You for the many good gifts You bestow, I affirm that You are the One from whom all blessings flow. Help me to thank You also in the midst of adversity—trusting in Your goodness *and* Your sovereignty.

Please teach me how to fill up the spare moments of my life with praise and thanksgiving. This joyous discipline will enable me to live in the intimacy of Your loving Presence.

IN YOUR PRAISEWORTHY NAME, JESUS, AMEN.

Thou art holy, O thou that inhabitest
the praises of Israel.

PSALM 22:3 KJV

Praise the LORD. Praise the LORD, my soul.
I will praise the LORD all my life; I will sing
praise to my God as long as I live.

PSALM 146:1–2

Give thanks in all circumstances, for this
is God's will for you in Christ Jesus.

1 THESSALONIANS 5:18

Glorious Savior,

I'm grateful that You are *in my midst* and You are mighty. Just as the sun is at the center of the solar system, *You* are at the center of my entire being—physical, emotional, and spiritual. You, *the Mighty One* who created the universe, live in me! I want to take time to absorb this amazing truth—letting it reverberate in my mind and soak into my innermost being.

I delight in pondering what it means to have so much Power dwelling within me. As I think about Your powerful Presence, I realize I don't need to worry about my lack of strength. Moreover, I'm comforted to know that *Your Power is completed and shows itself most effectively in my weakness.*

Jesus, please remind me frequently that You live in me and You are mighty! I ask that my awareness of Your indwelling Presence may drive out discouragement and fill me with Joy. I'm so thankful that Your Life flows into me continually, strengthening me with Your divine might.

In Your mighty Name, Jesus, Amen.

The Lord your God in your midst,
the Mighty One, will save.

ZEPHANIAH 3:17 NKJV

Now to him who is able to do immeasurably
more than all we ask or imagine, according
to his power that is at work within us.

EPHESIANS 3:20

My grace (My favor and loving-kindness and mercy) is
enough for you [sufficient against any danger and enables
you to bear the trouble manfully]; for My strength and
power are made perfect (fulfilled and completed) and
show themselves most effective in [your] weakness.

2 CORINTHIANS 12:9 AMPC

My faithful God,

I look to You this day for help, comfort, and companionship. I know You are always by my side, so even a glance can connect me with You. When I look to You for help, it flows freely from Your Presence. You are teaching me to recognize my constant need for You—in small matters as well as large ones.

When I need comfort, You lovingly enfold me in Your arms. You enable me not only to feel comforted but to be a channel through whom You comfort others. As a result, I am doubly blessed. While Your comfort is flowing through me to others, some of that blessing absorbs into me.

Your continual Companionship is an amazing gift! As I look to You, I find You faithful, true, and lovingly present with me. No matter what losses I may experience in my life, I know that *nothing can ever separate me from Your Loving Presence*!

In Your comforting Name, Jesus, Amen.

Those who look to him are radiant; their
faces are never covered with shame.

PSALM 34:5

The God of all comfort . . . comforts us in all our troubles,
so that we can comfort those in any trouble with the
comfort we ourselves have received from God.

2 CORINTHIANS 1:3–4

Nothing can ever separate us from God's love.
Neither death nor life, neither angels nor demons,
neither our fears for today nor our worries about
tomorrow—not even the powers of hell.

ROMANS 8:38–39 NLT

The more you focus on My Presence with you, the more fully you can enjoy life. Glorify Me through your pleasure in Me. Thus you proclaim My Presence to the watching world.

A Prayer for My Children

About the Author

Sarah Young, author of the bestselling 365-day devotionals *Jesus Calling®* and *Jesus Listens®*, was committed to helping people connect with Jesus and the Bible. Her books have sold more than 50 million copies worldwide. *Jesus Calling®* has appeared on all major bestseller lists. Sarah's writings include *Jesus Calling®*, *Jesus Listens®*, *Jesus Always*, *Jesus Today®*, *Jesus Lives*™, *Dear Jesus*, *Jesus Calling® for Little Ones*, *Jesus Calling® Bible Storybook*, *Jesus Calling®: 365 Devotions for Kids*, and more, each encouraging readers in their journeys toward intimacy with Christ. Sarah believed praying for her readers was a privilege and God-given responsibility and did so daily even amidst her own health challenges.

Connect with Jesus Calling at:
Facebook.com/JesusCalling
Instagram.com/JesusCalling
Youtube.com/JesusCallingBook
Pinterest.com/Jesus_Calling

Experience Peace in His Presence

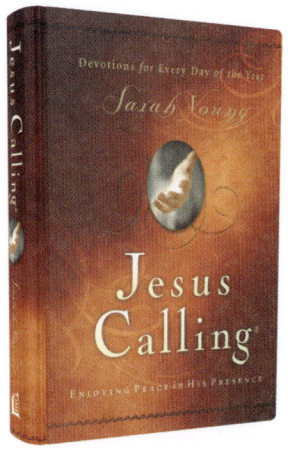

Written as if Jesus Himself is speaking directly to you—words of encouragement, comfort, and reassurance of His unending love.

Jesus Calling® is your yearlong guide to living a more peaceful life, delivering His message of love every day.

ISBN 978-1-5914-5188-4

I AM THE GIFT that continuously gives—bounteously, with no strings attached. Unconditional Love is such a radical concept that even My most devoted followers fail to grasp it fully. Absolutely nothing in heaven or on earth can cause Me to stop loving you.

—AN EXCERPT FROM *JESUS CALLING*®

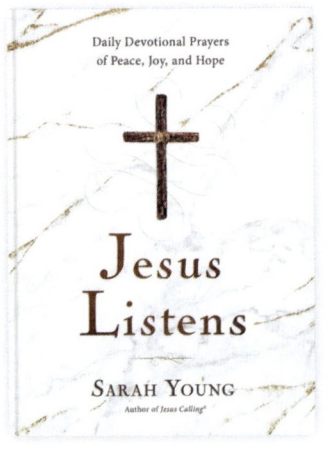

Find peace and hope in Jesus. This 365-day devotional prayer book from the author of *Jesus Calling*® gives you short, heartfelt prayers based on Scripture to deepen your connection to Him.

"Strong Savior,

Your Word assures me that You are both with me and for me. When I decide on a course of action that conforms to Your will, nothing can stop me. So I won't give up, even if I encounter multiple obstacles as I move toward my goal. I know there will be many ups and downs as I journey with You, but *with Your help* I can overcome any obstacle. I'm encouraged by the glorious truth that You, my *ever-present Help*, are omnipotent!"

—AN EXCERPT FROM *JESUS LISTENS*®